Bird

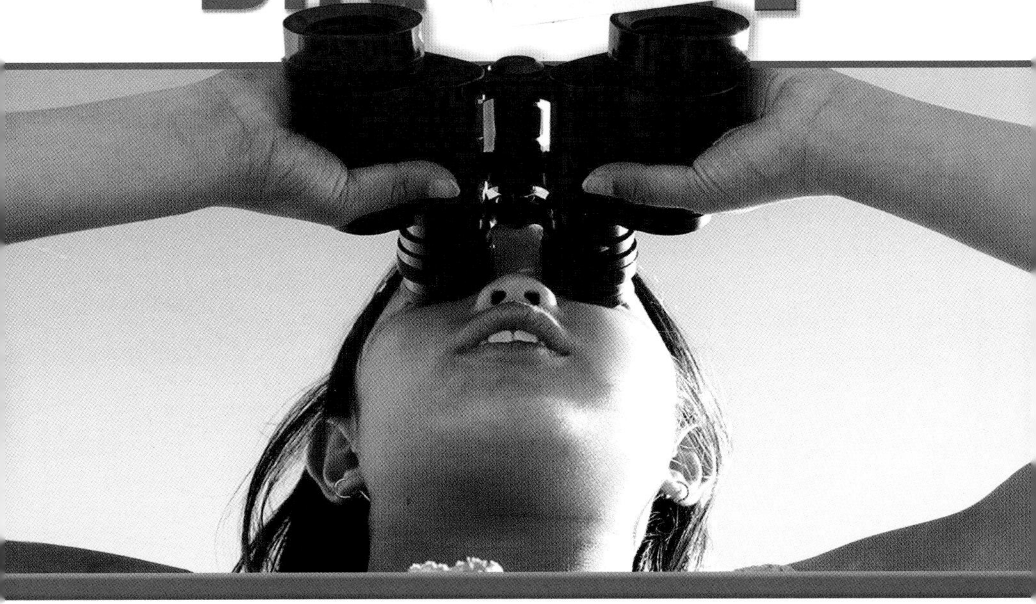

Rob Waring, *Series Editor*

HEINLE
CENGAGE Learning™

Australia • Brazil • Japan • Korea • Mexico • Singapore • Spain • United Kingdom • United States

Words to Know

This story is set in the U.S. state of Florida. It takes place in the city of Fort Lauderdale [fɔrt lɔdərdeɪl], which is on the coast of Florida, near the Atlantic Ocean.

A **A Special Girl.** Read the paragraph. Then match each word or phrase with the correct definition.

Mary Lou Robertson lives in Fort Lauderdale, Florida and has a very interesting hobby: bird-watching. In fact, she's so interested in birds that she has become an author and written a children's book about them. Every day, Mary Lou goes outside with her binoculars to watch the birds and other wildlife around her home. She often tracks birds through the forests and sometimes finds their young.

1. bird-watching _____
2. author _____
3. binoculars _____
4. wildlife _____
5. track _____
6. young _____

a. a person who writes a work (poem, story, etc.)
b. the practice of observing birds in their natural environment
c. the babies of animals
d. follow the movement of something
e. animals and birds living in their natural setting
f. special glasses that make distant objects appear closer

B **Coastal Birds.** Read the descriptions. Then write the number of the correct name next to each bird in the picture.

1. **Great Blue Heron:** very tall gray bird with white on face and yellow mouth
2. **Great Egret:** large white type of heron with yellow mouth and black legs
3. **Ibis:** large white bird with black under wings and pink mouth and legs
4. **mockingbird:** smaller songbird with gray body and some white on wings
5. **Osprey:** larger bird with brown wings, white body, and black on sides of head
6. **owl:** night bird with a hooked mouth, large eyes, and gray or brown body

The alarm clock rings in an average house on an average day in a neighborhood in Fort Lauderdale but there's nothing average about the young girl who is waking up in this house. Mary Lou Robertson is an experienced bird-watcher at a very young age. In fact, she's so knowledgeable about birds that she has already written a children's book about them. Not bad for a 13-year-old girl who is still in school!

So when did this young schoolgirl first become interested in bird-watching? It all started when her family moved to a new neighborhood. Mary Lou explains that she would feel very lonely at times when she first moved to her new home. She had left her friends behind when she moved, and on her new street there weren't many children to play with. Becoming a bird-watcher helped her to settle into the new neighborhood and to feel more at home. "[After] moving to a new neighborhood [without] many kids living on my street," she says, "the wildlife sort of brought me closer to feeling like I had friends."

CD 1, Track 09

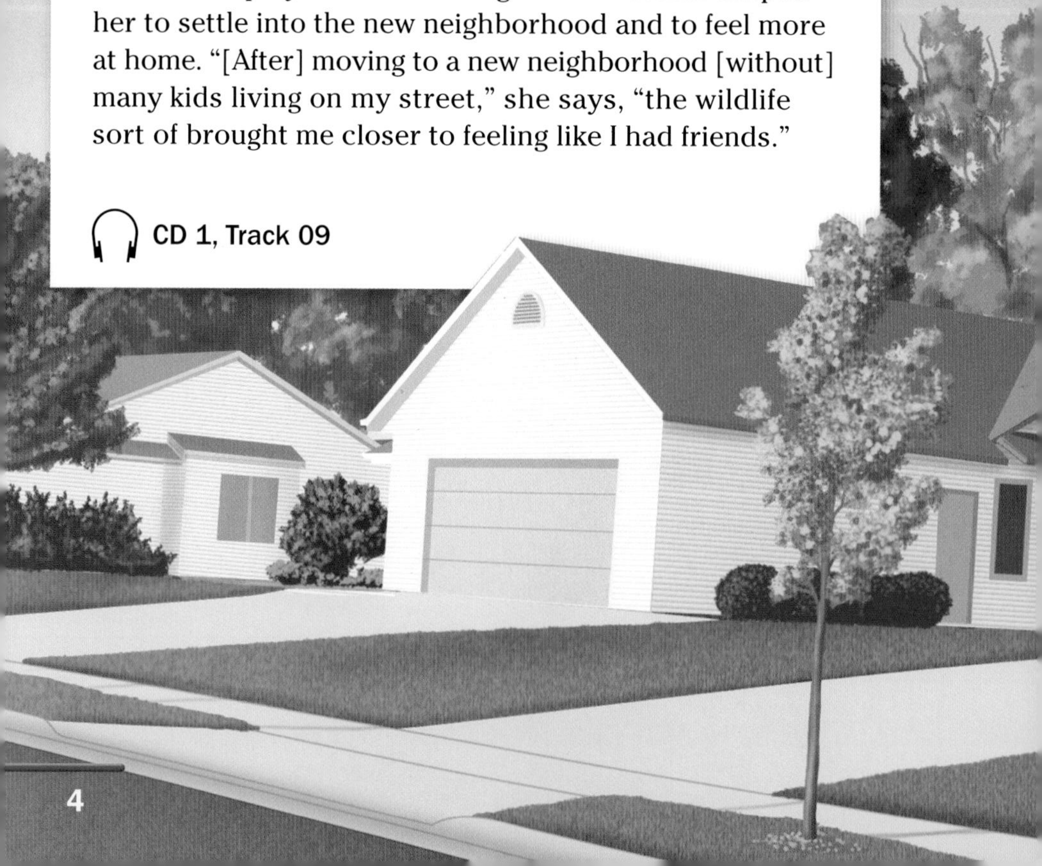

Scan for Information

Scan pages 7 and 8 to find the information.

1. What qualities does a bird-watcher need to possess?
2. What does Mary Lou use to identify birds?
3. How does Mary Lou's mother feel about her daughter's bird-watching?

Every morning Mary Lou takes her binoculars and heads out to look for birds. But what qualities do bird-watchers need? Mary Lou explains that in order to watch birds, one must be quiet and calm and not make a lot of noise. She says that if the watcher makes any sudden movements, the birds will probably become scared because they'll think that the person is a **predator**.[1]

Mary Lou usually uses her binoculars to identify all the different types of birds around her home. There are many varieties of birds for her to watch, and she never knows just what she might see. "Yeah," she says, excitedly as she sees a bird flying near her, "here comes one right now." As it passes by with a group of birds, she reports, "There goes an ibis. You can tell because they have black on the under part of their wings." It's clear that Mary Lou is quite an expert on the different types of birds.

---

[1]**predator:** an animal that lives by killing and eating others

What does Mary Lou's family think about her hobby? Mary Lou's mother, Mary Ellen, talks about her daughter's interest in bird-watching and how she has become such an expert. She seems to be really pleased that Mary Lou enjoys bird-watching so much and talks about how the interest started. "Well, she just seemed **intensively**[2] interested," she says. "And she just made it a part of her **routine**[3] to keep going out every day and looking and watching for signs of them and tracking them. It just seemed [to be] more than just a **casual**[4] interest."

---

[2]**intensively:** *(unusual use)* very; extremely
[3]**routine:** a series of things that someone does regularly
[4]**casual:** not very serious

Mary Lou first became very involved in bird-watching when she was in the sixth grade at St. Anthony's School in Fort Lauderdale, Florida. As part of a homework assignment, she was asked to write a book for a school project. At the time, she wondered about what she should write. Finally, she decided to write about something she knew, a bird that is locally famous: the mockingbird.

As she observes a mockingbird on a nearby rooftop, Mary Lou takes a moment to share some information about it. "The mockingbird is the state bird of Florida," she explains. "It protects its young until they fly away. I've seen it chase owls. Right now it's singing, but it will sometimes **yell**[5] at the other birds. It'll sound sort of like a cat **hissing**."[6] Luckily, writing about mockingbirds was just the beginning of Mary Lou's great writing adventure.

---

[5]**yell:** cry out loudly
[6]**hiss:** the noise a scared or angry cat makes

Mary Lou often spends time just sitting in wildlife areas and observing the various birds. She watches them closely as they come to eat or drink at a nearby pond. She describes her interest in birds, explaining that some birds, especially the larger ones, are simply beautiful to watch. "The first time I saw a Great Blue Heron and a Great Egret," she says, "they were beautiful sights because both of them are **majestic**,[7] slow-moving … very neat," she explains, and then adds, "They're beautiful to watch fly across water."

Many birds are easy for Mary Lou to identify, but she can't always name every bird she sees. Every day, there's a new lesson for Mary Lou to learn, a new bird to identify, and sometimes the sky is full of secrets.

---

[7]**majestic:** very beautiful and grand

A black skimmer skimming along the water.

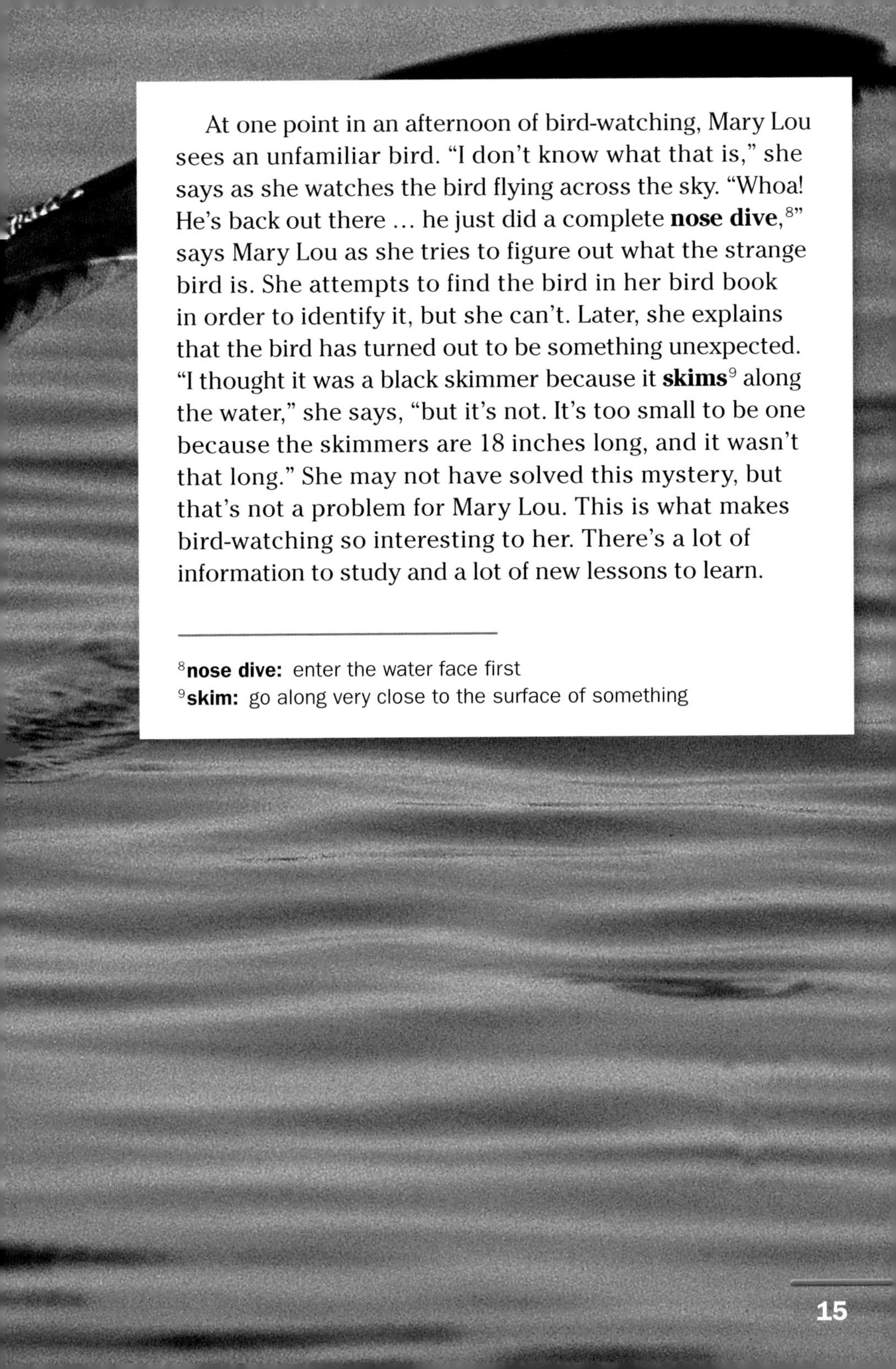

At one point in an afternoon of bird-watching, Mary Lou sees an unfamiliar bird. "I don't know what that is," she says as she watches the bird flying across the sky. "Whoa! He's back out there ... he just did a complete **nose dive**,[8]" says Mary Lou as she tries to figure out what the strange bird is. She attempts to find the bird in her bird book in order to identify it, but she can't. Later, she explains that the bird has turned out to be something unexpected. "I thought it was a black skimmer because it **skims**[9] along the water," she says, "but it's not. It's too small to be one because the skimmers are 18 inches long, and it wasn't that long." She may not have solved this mystery, but that's not a problem for Mary Lou. This is what makes bird-watching so interesting to her. There's a lot of information to study and a lot of new lessons to learn.

---

[8] **nose dive:** enter the water face first
[9] **skim:** go along very close to the surface of something

When Mary Lou was writing her bird book for children, she studied hard by searching the Internet. Initially, she needed as much information as she could find about each bird. She also drew and painted some of the birds for the book herself. Finally, after nine months of hard work, the book was finished.

Mary Ellen, Mary Lou's mother, was extremely proud of her daughter's achievement. She says, "I really felt like she really did **accomplish**[10] something, because she didn't just look at the birds, but she tried to interpret them for younger children." Mary Ellen then explains that her daughter tried to give the book more of a personal touch in order to help younger readers to become interested in the birds. "She did it in first person," explains Mary Ellen, "She gave the bird a personality [in order] to try to invite children to learn more about them."

---

[10]**accomplish:** achieve; manage to do something

Later, Mary Lou reads a short piece of text from her book. As she does so, the listener can hear how each piece tells a little about a bird and gives it a personality. "Hi, my name is Ossie the Osprey," she begins. "I live in rivers, lakes, and coastal waterways." She then continues with the next bird. "Hi, I'm Olivia the Owl," she reads, "I give six deep **hoots**."[11] The book is beautifully illustrated and both easy and interesting for children to read. The additional advantage with Mary Lou's book is that it is also educational.

It's unusual for a young girl to feel so strongly about a hobby. Has bird-watching changed Mary Lou at all? In many ways it hasn't changed her in the least; she still plays with her brother and sister and does the things that other children do. But since she became so involved with birds, something about her is slightly different. She explains in her own words: "Now I observe more of the world than I did when I was younger. I feel more attached. I feel that everything around me is important. I look at everything I can, because it might be something different than what I think it is." This young bird-watcher and author now knows that things aren't always what they appear to be. Each new thing she sees might be something exciting and different. For this curious young 'Bird Girl,' everything might just be another chance to learn something new!

[11] **hoot:** the noise that owls make

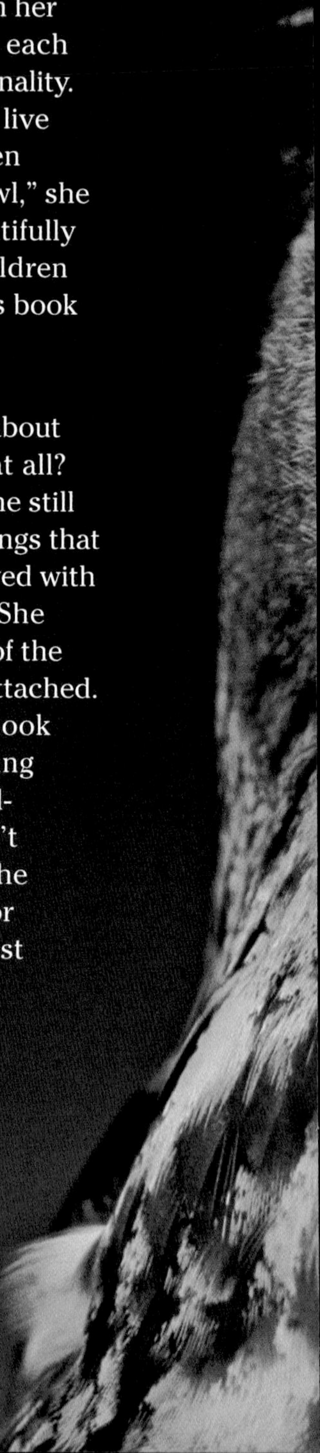

Infer Meaning

1. What does Mary Lou mean by 'I observe more of the world than I did when I was younger'?
2. What does she mean by 'it might be something different than what I think it is'?

After You Read

1. Why is Mary Lou Robertson an unusual girl?
A. She uses binoculars.
B. She likes wildlife.
C. She moved to a new neighborhood.
D. She is the author of a book about birds.

2. Bird-watching is a hobby that _________ can enjoy.
A. each
B. anyone
C. someone
D. even

3. In paragraph 2 on page 7, what is Mary Lou doing when she is speaking?
A. waking up
B. walking in her neighborhood
C. looking for birds
D. scaring wildlife

4. In paragraph 2 on page 7, to whom or to what does the word 'one' refer?
A. a flying bird
B. another bird-watcher
C. a sitting owl
D. a predator

5. Mary Lou does each of these every day EXCEPT:
A. tracks birds
B. gets up early
C. writes a book
D. enjoys her hobby

6. The mockingbird is:
A. Fort Lauderdale's city bird
B. majestic and slow moving
C. very quiet
D. protective of its young

7. On page 12, why is the 'sky full of secrets'?
A. Sometimes Mary Lou doesn't know all of the birds.
B. Owls sometimes chase mockingbirds.
C. Black skimmers are very long.
D. Majestic birds fly slowly over water.

8. On page 15, why does Mary Lou say 'Whoa!'?
A. because she is scared
B. because she is surprised
C. because she is angry
D. because she is happy

9. A suitable heading for page 15 is:
A. Mary Lou Sees a Black Skimmer
B. An Exciting Sighting
C. Bird-Watcher Makes a Mistake
D. Not Big Enough

10. Mary Lou's mother thinks her daughter is:
A. very outgoing
B. a quiet girl
C. a thoughtful writer
D. a beginner bird-watcher

11. What is the main idea in paragraph 2 on page 18?
A. Mary Lou likes birds.
B. Bird-watching has slightly changed Mary Lou.
C. Mary Lou has many different interests.
D. Mary Lou is good at many things.

12. What is the purpose of the story?
A. to tell about an unusual girl
B. to teach about birds in Florida
C. to show that bird-watching is fun
D. to show a mother is proud of her daughter

http://www.counting*birds.com

The Big Bird Count

States Reporting the Most Birds Last Year		
Rank	**State**	**Individual Birds Counted**
#1	New Jersey	657,150
#2	Florida	651,897
#3	Washington	563,457
#4	California	538,910
#5	Virginia	461,125
#6	Pennsylvania	417,200
#7	New York	414,618
#8	Texas	410,676
#9	Missouri	404,088
#10	Indiana	382,182

WHAT IS A 'BIRD COUNT'?

A bird count is an annual event in which people count the number of birds in their neighborhood. Local bird-watchers make lists of all the different types of birds they see, and how many of each type they see. Bird counts typically last for four days. During this period, groups of bird-watchers bring their binoculars and join their friends to explore the streets, parks, fields, and woods near their homes.

WHO CAN PARTICIPATE?

Everyone is welcome to take part in the event and no special skills are required. There are bird counters as young as seven and as old as ninety. Watchers only need to learn the names of the birds found in their area. There are plenty of bird books full of photographs to help newcomers identify the birds they see.

HOW DOES IT WORK?

Bird counters must first commit to spending at least 15 minutes counting birds for the survey. Then, they just need to walk around their community to record what they see on a Bird Count form. These forms may later be reported over the Internet. Counters can count birds in one place or in several locations. They can work alone or in a group, and can work for one day or for several days in a row. Any information that is collected and sent in is helpful.

WHY COUNT BIRDS?

Scientists need this information in order to track diseases and to study how climate changes may be affecting birds. They also use it to study how the growth of housing and manufacturing affects bird populations in an area. Scientists are especially interested in tracking birds that may be endangered, but they could never gather this much information by themselves. Each year, U.S. bird counters track over 600 different types of birds and complete about 80,000 surveys that report on 11 million individual birds!

"I thought bird-watching was a really strange idea until my class got involved. We did it as part of a unit on wildlife. I couldn't believe how much fun it was! At first, all the birds looked the same, but then I started to notice their beautiful colors and the unusual ways they move. It was amazing!"

Rico Martinez, 13
Corpus Christi, Texas

CD 1, Track 10

Word Count: 348
Time: _____

Vocabulary List